# DiRTY STOP OUTS GUIDE TO 1970s Barnsley

### By Nik Farah

Starring:

Club Ba-Ba

The Londoner

Trades Club

King George

The Birdcage

Stables

Changes

Old No 7

C000246251

Copyright © 2017 Nik Farah
**ISBN 978-1-908431-42-4**
All rights reserved. No part of this book may be reproduced in any form or by any electronic or mechanical means, including information storage or retrieval systems, without permission in
writing from the publisher, except by a reviewer who may quote brief passages.
Every effort has been made to trace the copyright holders of photographs in this book but one or two were unreachable. We would be grateful if the photographers concerned would contact us.

**Published by ACM Retro**
**Visit ACM Retro at:**
www.acmretro.com

Nik Farah asserts the moral right to be identified as the author of this work. A catalogue record for this book is available from the British Library. Other titles in this series:
Dirty Stop Out's Guide to 1970s Manchester (published November 2017).
Dirty Stop Out's Guide to 1970s Liverpool (published November 2017).
Dirty Stop Out's Guide to 1970s Coventry (published November 2017).
Dirty Stop Out's Guide to Working Men's Clubs (published October 2017).
Dirty Stop Out's Guide to 1950s Sheffield.
Dirty Stop Out's Guide to 1960s Sheffield.
Dirty Stop Out's Guide to 1970s Sheffield.
Dirty Stop Out's Guide to 1980s Sheffield.
Dirty Stop Out's Guide to 1990s Sheffield.
Dirty Stop Out's Guide to 1970s Chesterfield.
Dirty Stop Out's Guide to 1980s Chesterfield.
Dirty Stop Out's Guide to 1980s Chesterfield Quizbook.
We're on the look out for writers to cover other UK towns and cities and we're always on the look out for great retro photos! Please email is at
**info@dirtystopouts.com** if you fancy getting involved.

**www.dirtystopouts.com**

A 1970 donkey derby in Cawthorne

# Contents

A Tupperware fair at
The Queen's Hotel'

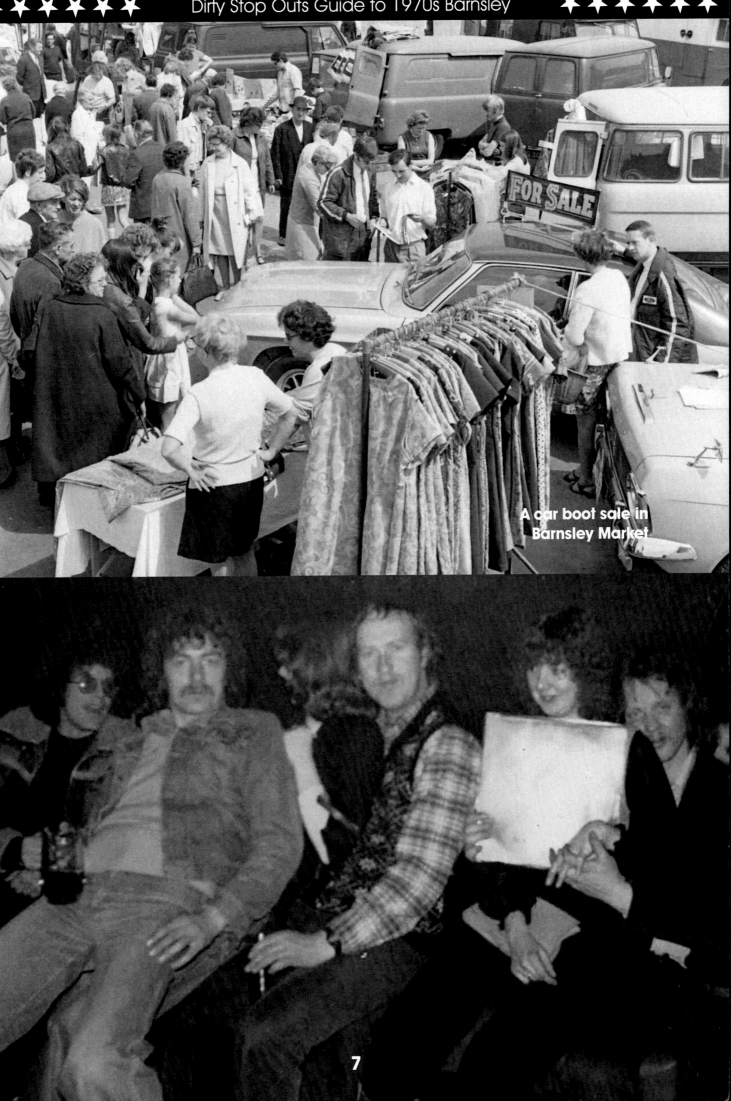

A car boot sale in
Barnsley Market

Fun and games at a gala in Dodworth

8

Ladies on the town at Club Ba-Ba

Students on a break from classes at Barnsley College

# Introduction
## Diving into Barnsley's decade of glam

❛These young people today think they invented misbehaving… they have no idea the kind of things we got up to!'

This quote, from Terry Dowle, is probably my favourite from the many chats and cups of tea I enjoyed with the good people of Barnsley in the course of compiling this book.

And how true the words are – from brawls over girls and money, police raids and court appearances, and partying with musicians and upcoming stars, to a beauty queen having to be rescued by the police from a locked club at 4am after falling asleep in a cubicle – there's no doubt the youth of 1970s Barnsley knew how to have a good time.

The 1970s was by all accounts a bright time for the northern mining town's 'young uns,' who were keen to dispel its 'cloth cap' reputation and inject a little glamour. Girls were no longer trekking to their nearest Coop to buy a suit and gloves, in an effort to emulate their mothers. Barnsley was being invaded by the same fashions and trends as the bigger cities, with influences ranging from Abba and *Saturday Night Fever* to Cher and the Bay City Rollers (tartan, anyone?). Big hair was the key – whatever your gender – and ladies everywhere were reaching for their round brushes, in an effort to recreate the perfect Farrah flick.

With Yorkshire Area NUM president Sam Bullough stating - in his 1973 New Year message - that 'the future of the coal industry is bright with promise,' miners were digging into their pockets and spending healthily on recreation and good times.

"The mines were going full pelt and life was good," said Joyce Beevers.

"The flat-cap image of Barnsley old was disappearing, and was in fact something of a sore point amongst us youngsters, as it gave way to something that was entirely more glam."

Local author and historian Dave Cherry confirmed: "It was a good time for Barnsley, with plenty of employment. I was working in the pits at the time, and I remember the miners' strikes of '72 and '74 well. The Tory PM did his best to blackmail the country with selected power strikes, hoping to turn public opinion against the trade unions, but it didn't work, and the miners won.

"Not as many people drove then, so there weren't as many cars on the road at that time, meaning that Barnsley was quite an insular place. People worked here, played here, and stayed here, and we all looked out for each other."

On January 1, 1973, Britain joined the EU, sliding into the Common Market 'quietly, and without a murmur or any fireworks,' according to an article in The Barnsley Chronicle, which labelled the change 'an anti-climax.' Closer to home, local beauty queen, Dorothy Hays, was leading the regional fight for flexitime, believing that workers should be able to choose their own hours. Everywhere you looked, people were taking a stand, or supporting a cause.

Pat Glover said: "There was a lot happening in the '70s in terms of music and empowerment, and it was all quite exciting.

❝ "We'd just had the swinging sixties, watching our older siblings leading the way and starting to change things, so when my generation came through in the '70s, we were the first generation where it was actually expected that we would do more – and we couldn't wait to do more!

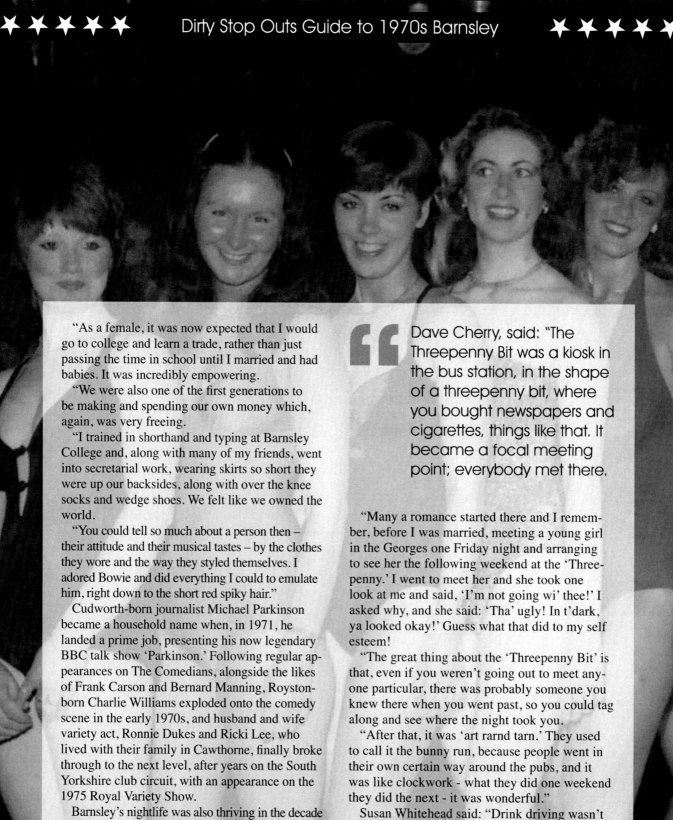

"As a female, it was now expected that I would go to college and learn a trade, rather than just passing the time in school until I married and had babies. It was incredibly empowering.

"We were also one of the first generations to be making and spending our own money which, again, was very freeing.

"I trained in shorthand and typing at Barnsley College and, along with many of my friends, went into secretarial work, wearing skirts so short they were up our backsides, along with over the knee socks and wedge shoes. We felt like we owned the world.

"You could tell so much about a person then – their attitude and their musical tastes – by the clothes they wore and the way they styled themselves. I adored Bowie and did everything I could to emulate him, right down to the short red spiky hair."

Cudworth-born journalist Michael Parkinson became a household name when, in 1971, he landed a prime job, presenting his now legendary BBC talk show 'Parkinson.' Following regular appearances on The Comedians, alongside the likes of Frank Carson and Bernard Manning, Royston-born Charlie Williams exploded onto the comedy scene in the early 1970s, and husband and wife variety act, Ronnie Dukes and Ricki Lee, who lived with their family in Cawthorne, finally broke through to the next level, after years on the South Yorkshire club circuit, with an appearance on the 1975 Royal Variety Show.

Barnsley's nightlife was also thriving in the decade of glam, with Changes and Stables a popular choice with the younger crowd, Keresforth Hall for a bit of sophistication, and Club Ba-Ba for star-studded cabaret and variety acts. Plus, of course hundreds of pubs and Workng Men's Clubs where hardworking men and women would flock, looking to shake things up at the end of a long week.

First dates, friends, boyfriends and girlfriends would meet at the 'Threepnny Bit' newsstand in the bus station, before heading on to The Royal, Old No 7, King George or The Fitz to start their night.

❝❞ Dave Cherry, said: "The Threepenny Bit was a kiosk in the bus station, in the shape of a threepenny bit, where you bought newspapers and cigarettes, things like that. It became a focal meeting point; everybody met there.

"Many a romance started there and I remember, before I was married, meeting a young girl in the Georges one Friday night and arranging to see her the following weekend at the 'Threepenny.' I went to meet her and she took one look at me and said, 'I'm not going wi' thee!' I asked why, and she said: 'Tha' ugly! In t'dark, ya looked okay!' Guess what that did to my self esteem!

"The great thing about the 'Threepenny Bit' is that, even if you weren't going out to meet anyone particular, there was probably someone you knew there when you went past, so you could tag along and see where the night took you.

"After that, it was 'art rarnd tarn.' They used to call it the bunny run, because people went in their own certain way around the pubs, and it was like clockwork - what they did one weekend they did the next - it was wonderful."

Susan Whitehead said: "Drink driving wasn't something anyone worried about, you wouldn't think anything of having a few drinks and then driving through to Wakefield for last orders, as unbelievable as that seems now.

"We never went out on a mission to get absolutely legless though, like so many young people do now, it's not what it was about for us. We went out to socialise and have fun with our friends.

"It was a special 'lightning in a bottle' kind of time that I don't think we'll ever see repeated."

**Beauty contestants
line up at Rebecca's
nightclub**

Yvonne Tingle could have had no idea how much a mis-labeled caption in the local newspaper would screw up her social life.

The 22-year-old contacted The Barnsley Chronicle in April 1970 after her photo ran in the paper with another person's name under it, mistakenly leading people to believe she was married.

Before the error, two years earlier, Yvonne claimed she was being 'dated as many as five times a week.' But all that was to change, following the misprint, which eventually drove Yvonne to make the public declaration with a half-page story, headlined: 'I'm Miss not Mrs, proclaims Yvonne.'

"It is getting beyond a joke," the Kendray woman was quoted as saying.

"The last time I had a date was Christmas, and people are always asking me how I am going on now I am married."

Yvonne's mother, Mrs Connie Tingle, added: "This rumour that Yvonne is married is getting her down. She used to have lots of boyfriends, but she seems out of it now."

YVONNE TINGLE

# I'M MISS NOT MRS. PROCLAIMS YVONNE

Y VONNE TINGLE, 22-YEARS-OLD SUPERVISOR IN A CHEMIST'S SHOP IN BARNSLEY, WANTS IT MADE PUBLIC THAT SHE IS A MISS.

The story has got around that Yvonne, from Swanee Road, Kendray, is married. "But believe me, the way things are carrying on I never will be," she said this week.

It all started two years ago when her picture appeared in the paper with another woman's name under it.

At that time she was being dated as many as five times a week.

"Now all that's changed," she said. "I never have any decent boy friends, and I have only had about five dates in the last year."

"It is getting beyond a joke. The last time I had a date was Christmas, and people are always asking me how I am going on now I am married."

Yvonne's mother, Mrs Connie Tingle said: "This rumour that Yvonne is married is getting her down. She used to have lots of boy friends, but she seems out of it now."

It was May 19, 1974, when Julie Healey found herself at Barnsley Civic Theatre, along with youngsters from all across the region, for a sold-out performance by the Bay City Rollers, which saw queues starting hours before showtime.

"I went to school with the Civic manager John Simmon's daughter, so there was no queue for our group," she recalled.

"I don't remember a whole lot about it now, but I do still remember the tartan trousers that I wore!"

Pat Glover during her 'David Bowie' phase

A night out at Rebecca's nightclub in the late 70s

Keith Adams at his
21st birthday party

A Coal Queen meeting
with the Mayor and
Mayoress of Barnsley

Maureen
Hackett and
a colleague
at work

Barnsley Odeon

Yorkshire's first
female manager,
Barnsley girl Linda
Hammond, at a
local Ladbrokes

Yet another beauty contest, at The Bailey nighclub
in Monk Bretton Social Club, in 1970

**Mining advert from the Barnsley Chronicle**

**The tables in the casino at Ba-Ba**

# Chapter 1
## Betting, brawls and Ba-rilliant fun

**A**hh Club Ba-Ba...

Throughout most of the 1970s, Ba-Ba was the place to see and be seen in Barnsley; the very definition of good times in the decade of glam.

"Everyone went to the Ba-Ba," confirmed Chris Evans, who was assistant manager for a couple of years early on in the '70s.

"There was a strict dress code - you certainly wouldn't be admitted without a jacket and tie. The ladies often wore evening dresses, and some of the younger girls would wear mini skirts or hot pants."

Open seven nights a week, and with a full complement of staff that included resident dancers, croupiers, a compere, stagehands, and cocktail waitresses, the club was a little piece of big city glitz right in the centre of the South Yorkshire town.

The club had been launched by the well-known hypnotist Peter Casson in the late '60s, in the Magnet Bowl on Queen's Road, and was considered a 'real theatre nightclub,' that came close to competing with the neighbouring big boys of Batley Variety Club and Club Fiesta. It was the sister club to Club Ki-Ki in Doncaster's Kirk Sandall - also owned by Peter – and quickly gained a reputation for its star-studded cabaret.

"I remember seeing Johnnie Ray, The Rocking Berries, Ronnie Dukes and Ricki Lee, and The Grumbleweeds there," Chris recalled.

> "The culture of variety wasn't an entirely new thing for Barnsley, where lots of the WMCs also had live acts, but the Ba-Ba really was another level.

"It ran a full variety show at that time – five or six acts a night, including the top bill, and at least two sets from the resident dancers. Master of ceremonies Denis Lake was always resplendent in his tuxedo."

After depositing coats – and for many of the ladies, swapping their 'street' shoes for evening shoes – in the cloakroom ("Flimsy shoes were no good for walking through the streets of Barnsley," Chris noted), customers took their seats down by the stage or upstairs in the restaurant, which looked out over the main floor. For those who arrived too late to find a seat, there was standing room alongside two giant bars. The 'thrust' stage meant the audience enveloped performers on three sides, guaranteeing good views for all.

The popular casino also had its own bar, in a separate room behind the auditorium, and upstairs was The Frungle Room, which in 1970 was equipped with a large colour television, to screen the World Cup. Colour TV was still a fairly rare thing at that time and the Frungle Room was really popular during the Cup competition, but swiftly faded in popularity after that.

Maureen Lawford, then Maureen Hackett, still gets recognised to this day as 'the Ba-Ba lass' after a two-year stint as the club's resident dancer, from '70 to '72.

"I performed seven nights a week, it was the best job in the world and I have so many good memories," said Maureen.

"I'd rehearse through the day with the visiting act, and then be back at the club at 7pm. I'd do a bit of everything; tap, jazz, modern, either on my own or with the compere, Denis Lake, who was a great guy.

"I remember once doing this snake charmer routine and my bikini top coming unhooked halfway through. I managed to finish the routine with one arm, as I held my top up with the other. Afterwards, Denis told the audience that I'd been on the verge of giving them the entire Eastern Promise!"

And the glamorous blonde, aged just 18 when she started at the club, earned her fair share of admirers.

"Don Fardon claimed to have fallen in love with me, and I got serenaded by Solomon King," she laughed.

"The owner Peter Casson offered to take me out too, and Toni Christie used to tell me I looked like Clodagh Rodgers.

Gerry Marsden once gave me a lift home, to the amazement of my mum, who was one of his biggest fans at that time. I'll never forget her face, when I arrived home in the early hours in this maroon Bentley, with a gold GM on the side, and she came out to see what was going on. I thought she was going to faint when Gerry got out of the car!

"Another time I was bopping about with Russ Abbott and he spun me around, then as I went to grab his hand again, he dropped his trousers. He was a funny guy."

Though not all the acts she appeared with were as pleasant as Gerry and Russ.

"I was once backstage with Long John Baldry who was wearing this very expensive-looking jacket. I told him I liked it, running my hand down an embroidered sleeve, at which point he recoiled – as if I'd burned him – and hissed 'don't touch!'"

And another thing Maureen remembers all too well are the stories of the Ba-Ba ghost.

"It was Russ Abbott that first mentioned the ghost to me," she recalled.

"It was said to be some guy who'd been killed on

**Peter Casson's co-owner, Jack Lister**

the building site of the bowling alley next door. This one day I came into my dressing room, which I always kept locked, and the room had been ransacked, with sheet music, make-up and shoes everywhere. Quite a few people thought that was the ghost's handiwork..."

Beverley Ann Beevers, whose mum Joyce was the club's promoter throughout the '70s, said: "I remember my mum zooming around in her blue Triumph Spitfire promoting the best nightspot in the north.

"Visiting celebrities would often stay at the Rockingham Villas. My siblings and I met many of them there.

"I loved hearing my mum's stories of the séances held in the casino when it was closed!"

Her mum Joyce added: "I would go to factories and offices in the day, in my little white skirt and white boots, to promote Ba-Ba. It was such a great place.

"There was a girl called Eileen who worked on reception and everyone called her 'legs' because she would wear these short skirts which showed off her amazing legs.

"The dress code was quite strict and the owners, Peter Casson and Jack Lister liked it that way, as they said it kept the rabble out!"

Gavin Moore said: "I only went there once and was turned away for wearing a leather jacket."

The beautiful Ba-Ba
resident dancer,
Maureen Hackett

## Menu

DEEP FRIED SCAMPI ... 50p

ROAST SPRING CHICKEN 37½p

PLAICE GOUJON ... ... 37½p

Served with French Fried Potatoes
at your Table

★  ★

A LA CARTE MENU AVAILABLE IN OUR
RESTAURANT

FORTHCOMING
ATTRACTIONS
AT
CLUB BA-BA

Week commencing 5/4/71
GERRY MARSDEN

Week commencing 12/4/71
JOHN BALDRY

Week commencing 19/4
THE FORTUNE

Week commencing 26/
VANITY FAIR

Week commencing 3
JOHNNIE NE
STARLINERS

BITTER SU

Week commencing
JOE DOLA

## CLUB BA-BA

BARNSLEY 2112
Mon. 5 to Sat. 10 April
Peter Casson Presents

**GERRY MARSDEN**
(ex "Pacemakers")
Ian Kent : Ann Phillips : Mark Sebastian
Denis Lake & Maureen

MONDAY 5th APRIL
Chef's Cold Buffet, 15p

SUNDAYS ONLY 7-11.30 p.m. DISCO BA-BA
plus Jimmy James & the Vagabonds
**FREE** Chefs Cold Buffet included in
normal admission charges.
PARTY BOOKINGS-MEALS 50p.

In 'Life After Kes,' by Simon W Goulding, actor and comedian Duggie Brown is quoted as saying: 'I remember taking Tony Garnett to the Ba-Ba, and the bouncers wanted to shave Tony's sideburns off before they let him in. It was a rule – no long sideburns, but when I explained who he was, they reluctantly agreed.'

Chris Hanson worked at Club Ba-Ba as a lighting technician initially, before taking on the role of DJ for around six months: "I always played *'where peaceful waters flow,'* by Gladys Knight at 2am as the final song of the night."

Terry Dowle said: "The restaurant upstairs at Ba-Ba was absolutely brilliant, great food and a great view of the stage below."

Denis Wagstaff said: "I didn't have enough money to play the gaming tables, but I remember seeing great acts like Vanity Fayre, Chicory Tip, New World, and the late Dustin Gee. Fond memories."

> Anne Turton, who worked on the bar, recalled: "There were lots of Ba-Ba parties after hours...wild days and wilder nights!

The staff were all super people, some of the best times of my life."

Susan Whitehead said: "Ba-Ba really got going about 10pm, so my friends and I would always meet in The Royal first, then walk down. You had to be a member at Ba-Ba, or be signed in by one, but my friend Hilary and I were complimentaries, so we always got to walk in straight past the queue of people waiting outside.

"The acts were great – comedy acts, music acts, variety acts – they all came here; you could see anybody you wanted to at Ba-Ba."

Maria Lane said: "I remember once going to Ba-Ba in a paper dress – and it split! I was so embarrassed!"

Lynda Seddon said: "A night out at the Ba-Ba was the highlight of the week."

Pauline Lesley Mastro said: "It was the place to dance the night away," and Jean Sanderson added: "The days of Ba-Ba really were THE days!"

Ann Kennedy worked the club for over a decade, and says even the more upmarket clientele didn't stop fights from breaking out: "At the end of the day, Barnsley is a mining town with a mining mentality; there were lots of tough guys and lots of fights, usually over girls or money," she said.

"I remember people being carried out without their shoes and socks on, as the bouncers said that was the best way to take the fight out of anyone."

Karen Halford said: "My mum used to go there and she told me that one night she got thrown out, and her beehive hairpiece came off in the bloke's hand as he marched her out!"

Pamela Emson said: "I worked at Ba-Ba for a year or so in the casino and we would often go out after work to the Five Acres in Brierley. One night, the casino manager had his car broken into and his sheepskin coat was stolen...luckily the thieves missed the casino takings that were locked in the boot!"

Ann Kennedy added: "It wasn't an easy place for an act to perform, as a Barnsley audience is a tough crowd. I remember telling Rolf Harris to his face

**Playing in the casino at Club Ba-Ba (left), Ba-Ba's croupier staff enjoy a night out (right), a packed New Year's Eve dance floor at Club Ba-Ba (background),**

once, after he came off, that he'd been absolutely rubbish. He didn't like that much!

"The Searchers were practically booed offstage, and I remember Shirley Bassey came to audition for Jack Lister, but he said she had a potty mouth and needed to clean her act up before he'd have her on!"

And Ann also remembers the Ba-Ba being raided by the police, who closed them down for not having a gaming licence for the casino.

"But we did have a licence," insisted Ann.

"All of the croupier staff had to appear at Barnsley Magistrates, but it was just somebody stirring up trouble. I don't know where they got that idea from.

"I wagged my finger at the judge and told him he couldn't tell us we were doing anything illegal, as we had a gambling licence. People around me were sinking in their seats, but I was right and the judge knew it, so that was that!"

But sadly, a change to the legislation meant that Ba-Ba did indeed go on to lose its gambling licence in the 70s, and it was to be the reason for the club's eventual downfall.

Chris Evans said: "Maintaining a full variety programme without the casino subsidising the hiring of acts became impossible."

Ann confirmed: "Ba-Ba was never the same after that."

The club eventually closed in 1976, but what's clear is that, for a while there, in its heyday, Ba-Ba truly defined all that was young and glam about this exciting era, and remains an important chapter in Barnsley's history.

**Ba-Ba adverts from the Barnsley Chronicle**

Barnsley's Ba-Ba Club even got a mention in the autobiography of the late Paul Daniels who lived in a caravan in the nearby village of Cawthorne for a while in the '70s, and was a regular visitor and performer.

'Early on in the never-ending cycle of gigs, I met one of the greatest stage hypnotists I had ever seen, Peter Casson, who became my manager. We met because I got a week at the Club Ba-Ba in Barnsley, which he owned. I learnt a really big lesson on my first night there. I didn't think that I had gone down very well at all and I fully understood the large sign that Peter had put up backstage: 'Will all Artistes please refrain from asking the audience whether they are having a good time or enjoying themselves as the lack of response is invariably embarrassing to both parties.'

'As soon as I came offstage, the compere said that I was one of the funniest men ever to appear in the club, but the only thing I ought to do is slow up, as the rhythm of speech is much slower around Barnsley. Fabulous advice.'

Roy Phillips, of The Peddlers, said: "The Peddlers were once at Ba-Ba doing a gig, and the club was packed, but Peter Casson had a strict rule against epaulets. Unfortunately, our drummer, Trevor, was wearing epaulets and was refused entry! Peter said: 'I don't care who you are, you're not wearing epaulets in my club.' We were the main act that night and it really seemed like he wasn't going to let our drummer in!

"In the end, I went up to the front desk to talk to Peter, who finally relented and let Trevor in, so the show could go on. The Peddlers would have been a duo that night if Peter Casson had had his way!"

CLUB
Ba-Ba

WINING · DINING · DANCING

Ann Kennedy and
friend at Club Ba-Ba

A rare exterior shot
of the club, located
in the Magnet Bowl
on Queen's Road

Resident dancers
onstage at Club Ba-Ba

# Chapter 2

## From the Birdcage and the Stables:
## a Barnsley pub crawl!

**❝❝I was 16 when I started work as a clerk in Halifax Building Society on Market Hill, in 1971,"** recalled Frank Higham.

"My first wage slip for a month was £32.30. I handed £16 of it to my mum for board, which left me £16 to live on – and I felt rich!

"Barnsley was a great place to be young in the '70s – enjoying the music and the lifestyle. Very few people had phones, so you would just head out to the King George and there was always someone in there you knew.

❝❝ "I think one big difference was the strength of beer in those days - you got full before you were incapable, and it was hard to get into trouble when you had ten pints of beer sloshing around inside you.

"The King George was great as a meeting place. The cellar bar at the No.7, the Bodega and the White Hart were always full of people you knew."

Mal Remington recalls sneaking into the King George for a beer and lime before he was old enough.

"We knew it was risky, but we loved it," he said.

"That is until one day, my dad caught me sneaking out and grounded me for a month."

Lynda Seddon agreed: "It was the best decade of my life. I have wonderful memories of meeting up with friends at the 'Threepenny Bit,' all dressed up in the very latest fashion.

❝❝ "As a student nurse, I worked long hours and couldn't wait for my nights off when I would let my hair down, put on a pair of hot pants and knee length suede boots and spend the night dancing."

"Everyone would head for the King George pub on Peel Street and congregate to decide where to go, usually wherever there was a live band playing.

"I remember being in the Georges one night when a crew came in filming for 'Kes.' I was too shy to be filmed, but if you look carefully you can see me walking away in one of the shots that made the cut.

Of the town's many pubs and clubs at this time, two of the biggest and most popular were undoubtedly Changes, the former Alhambra pub, on Sheffield

**Fun and games during
a Marlboro promotion
at Rebeccas**

Road; and The Stables, previously The Hub on Peel Street.

Caroline Humphreys laughed: "I remember getting dragged out of Changes by my mum when I was 16, bearing in mind you had to be 21 to get into a night-club at that point!"

Terry Dowle said: "Changes was pretty good, we'd go there from time to time. It wasn't upmarket, like Club Ba-Ba, but it was more intimate."

Joyce Beevers added: "I never liked Changes, I remember you'd stick to the floor in that place."

Stuart Williams, who DJ'd at The Stables in the 1970s, said: "My life during this period consisted in the main of clubs, clubs and more clubs. I frequented Stables most nights, mainly because the owner had two fit daughters!

"I had previously run a mobile disco with a mate of mine, and so the owner of Stables started asking me to cover the DJ box on Friday nights. It was a bit daunting really, because it was a proper professional set-up with a few hundred boozed-up punters! I was more or less given free reign on what I could play, but kept it to mainstream music, always going into the record shop in Queen Street at Friday teatime, to buy the very latest releases to play Friday night. I also encouraged the crowd to bring in their own music for me to play, which kept them happy and kept my money in my pocket.

"My mate Tom and I introduced a Monday night Northern Soul night between 1971 and 1972, which unfortunately did not attract as many punters as we had wished, but we loved the music, and it was like having our very own disco every week. Great times."

Molly Logstaff added: "I remember The Stables very well, working there from 1972 to 1974. It's still one of the best jobs I ever had."

Wayne Powell said:

> "It was always Stables for the music, Ba-Ba for the chicken in a basket, and Changes for a dance and a scrap!"

Dave Cherry said: "The Cross Keys is where everyone finished up, as it was only a stone's throw to the buses from there. Last orders were 10.20pm and my last bus back to Worsbrough was 10.40pm, so it was a case of sup up and run!"

Susan Whitehead added: "The pubs in Barnsley at that time quite famously closed at half ten, whereas Wakefield was 11pm, so you'd have your last drink in a Barnsley pub at 10.30pm, then you'd see everyone charge off to the nearest pub they could get to between Barnsley and Wakefield, to squeeze another drink in before 11pm."

One venue Susan will never forget is the Bailey Nightclub in the old Monk Bretton Social Club,

which became The Londoner later in the 70s. The former Miss Brook Motors arrived at the club one night in 1970, dressed in a sparkly catsuit, having relinquished her crown and title at a big party at The Arcadian ballroom earlier in the evening.

"I remember that Bob Monkhouse was on that night," said Susan.

"My sister Kathryn was working in the cloakroom so I handed her my floor length coat and went to have some more champagne; it had been a great night.

> "The next thing I knew, I was waking up in the toilets in the pitch black at 4am. It turned out I'd fallen asleep and everybody was gone and the doors were locked!

"Luckily I knew where the office was, so I made my way through the dark rooms and up the stairs, found the phone and called the police. They had to come and let me out, but I was quite surprised when, rather than take me home, they took me to the police station, and confiscated my handbag."

It turned out that, while Susan was asleep in one of the cubicles, the club, off Lamb Lane in Monk Bretton, had been broken into and ransacked.

"Somebody had smashed into and stolen all the change from the cigarette machines, so the police wanted to check my tiny evening bag to see if I was

Hitting the dance floor at Rebecca's, with DJ Phil Jay in the box

John Renshaw said: "On Sunday afternoons they had strippers and comedians on, and coaches used to come from as far as Lancashire, so the place was packed out. The good old days."

Kath Kershaw said: "This was my favourite pub ever; I used to love the soul nights with Gary 'Bub' Buttle, he was a brilliant DJ."

Annemarie Lowe said: "My mate's mum worked there and we used to try and sneak in and watch Bub. I have great memories of that place."

'We Are Barnsley' presenter, Tommy Taylor, who worked at The Londoner in the '70s, said: "Weekends at The Londoner were very popular, playing the chart music of the time and a big section of Northern Soul which was at its most popular in the mid seventies.

"Monday night was dedicated Northern Soul night with Barnsley's very own legendary soul DJ Bub."

Stuart Williams said: "It was a really unique place, in that one week you could have Jimmy Ruffin, from Motown fame, appearing and the next week it could be Bob Monkhouse."

Claire Middleton said: "The roller discos there were brilliant too!"

Adrian Brear remembers playing pool with his friend Andrew one night in the poolroom at The Londoner when a group of girls came in, and changed the channel on the TV, that had been playing sports, sank into some chairs, and proceeded to watch an episode of The Waltons.

It wasn't until years later, while reminiscing about the incident, with his now-wife Hazel, that Hazel revealed she had been one of those girls!

"I had my first drink there, a Black Russian," said Alison Banham.

"I was 15, oops…."

And while The Friendship Inn in Gawber made a name for itself - with topless go-go girls every Monday - over in Hoyland, The Birdcage, with it's exotic palm trees and pink mood lighting, was the perfect place for locals to walk to (and stumble home from) on a summer's night.

"1976 was a mad hot summer that seemed to last forever," said Sandra Price.

"My local jaunts were all around Hoyland, where there were some good pubs, before heading down to The Birdcage to finish the evening off.

"Because I was lucky enough to come from a small village, there was always someone to see you home safe with no ulterior motive!"

Lynn Cooper agreed: "I used to love The Birdcage in the late '70s. It was great, so different and much better than the nightclubs down south. The palm trees added to the ambience and the atmosphere was great. I will always have my memories of fab nights grooving away in there.

"No need to fork out on taxis either back then, just as easy to stumble back down the hill in my white stilettos."

managing to hide a machine full of change in there!"

The Monk Bretton club also famously had its very own ghost, 'Old Joe,' that had haunted the establishment for a number of years, according to staff and local residents, who reported everything from sightings of 'a shadowy figure dressed as a Quaker of yesteryear' to 'hearing religious music being played on the organ at times when the club was closed and no organist was about.'

And this hugely popular club, which would meet its sad demise just a few years later, burning to the ground, is also well known as the place where film star Diana Dors broke her ankle when she visited the town in 1973.

According to a story in The Barnsley Chronicle at the time, Miss Dors had been paying a private visit to the club, whilst in the area to perform at the Wakefield Theatre Club, and had slipped and fractured her ankle, and had to be taken to Barnsley Beckett Hospital for an operation.

Jan Mills said: "There were so many top acts on at The Londoner, I have really happy memories, and was so sad when it burned down."

Tony Pointon recalled: "The Hilton twins, Albert and Jimmy, looked after the door at The Londoner and I remember the lead singer of Showaddywaddy got a bit lairy with them over parking his car one night, and there was a right set to - a good night had by all."

Jo Beevers added: "Good God the Hilton Twins! Monk Bretton's answer to the Krays! I loved that place!"

**Joyce Beevers on a rare night off, at Keresforth Hall**

**A resident dancer dances in among the palm trees of The Birdcage, in Hoyland**

**Lads larking around on a night out**

### Diana Dors breaks ankle at local club

Miss Dors' spot for the rest of the week, but nothing concrete at the moment.

The blonde actress is currently appearing on Yorkshire T.V. in a Wednesday evening half-hour comedy show called "All Our Saturdays."

She plays the manager of a works Rugby League team.

Diana Dors is in Barnsley Beckett Hospital today.

**Barnsley College students take to the town**

26

Yet another beauty queen is crowned

Hitting the dance floor at Rebeccas

The Birdcage at Hoyland

PRICE LIST

THE Birdcage NITESPOT

FRIENDSHIP INN
GAWBER, BARNSLEY
**TOPLESS GO-GO GIRLS**
PLUS DISCO
EVERY MONDAY
THURSDAY TO SUNDAY
**DISCO**
EVERY NIGHT
featuring
THE AREA'S TOP DISCOS

Bouncers on the door of The Birdcage, in Hoyland

Michael Keane and pals who could often be found at The Fitz, or The Georges

**Pulling out the beautiful girls and a big motorcycle to promote Marlboro**

**Fun and games during a Marlboro promotion at Rebeccas**

**Susan Whitehead pictured the night she relinquished her Miss Brook Motors crown… and ended up locked overnight in The Bailey nightclub!**

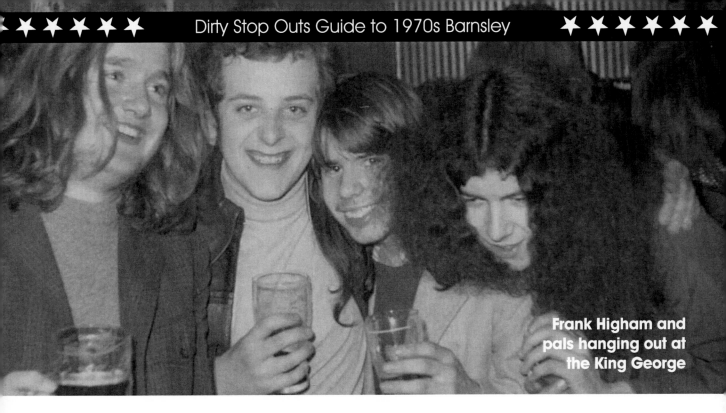

**Frank Higham and pals hanging out at the King George**

# Chapter 3
## Trendies vs hippies - and the explosion of the small town folk scene

With the arrival of the '70s, and the many changes it provoked, the mentality of this small town seemed to be changing too. There were distinct divisions between the 'trendies' and the 'hippies' and the town's folk clubs suddenly became a 'cool' alternative on a Saturday night.

Jason White, who runs the website 'Alternative Barnsley,' said: "In terms of Barnsley music of that period, folk was strong, with first albums from club organisers Dave Burland, and Derek and Dorothy Elliot, and popular folk clubs at Alhambra and the King George Hotel.

"You also had the hard blues bands, which were a precursor to heavy metal. The main one was The Iron Mad Wilkinson Band, which had Saxon singer Biff Byford and a local folky Don Garforth. You also had the first punk band, The Restricted, and later X-Rippers and Total Confusion.

"You also had the start of the anarcho-punk/squat scene, and the band Passion Killers, whose members went on to form Chumbawamba."

Barnsley bard Ian McMillan started performing his poetry in the 1970s on Barnsley's folk club scene and remembers it as a great time in the town.

"The folk clubs at that time were the best place for me," said Ian.

"People could get up and sing sea shanties, or read poetry, whatever they wanted. It was a bit like an alternative open mic night.

"I remember performing at the Centenary Rooms

folk club, The Wheatsheaf, the old King George – places like that accepted lads like me.

 The '70s were experimental, there were all kinds of things happening and suddenly it was alright to be doing something different.

"Me and some of my mates started a band in the '70s too - that's what you do when you're a youngster isn't it? I played drums, but I didn't have any drums at first, so I used to play on Tupperware; I really was the world's worst drummer! I remember we got a gig at Eldon Street Youth Club and some kids stole our fiddle.

"My girlfriend at the time, now my wife, and I would spend our Saturday nights going out to various folk clubs, seeing different acts on the stand-up scene. That was how I learned to do it myself. Wath Folk Club was the biggest one at that time, and the only time I ever got ill through drink was at a festival at Wath Folk Club. There was a woman there called Lindsay Lennon, who was the folk correspondent for the South Yorkshire Times, and she wrote in her column that she saw me being sick outside. So my mum's reading this and said to me 'you don't drink, do you Ian?' and so I told her it was a dodgy cheeseburger. So then I had to get the South Yorkshire Times to print a retraction the following week!

"For many of us, those years were some of the best of our lives. The world seemed to be moving on, changing with the times, but perhaps adolescents always think that."

Linda Hammond recalled: "I remember getting absolutely paralytic on barley wine one night, and walking home hugging all the lamp posts on the way!

"I loved the Fitz, the King George, the Royal, and on the odd occasion my friends and I would go to the White Hart or Alhambra."

Jim Sheridan said: "The slightly more mature hippies went on to The Fitzwilliam on Sackville Street, across from the art school, by whose students it was largely populated. There was a threepenny bit jukebox on one side of the bar, with righteous rock 'n' roll, and darts on the other side.

"Owners Arthur and Margaret Palmer were most cool and caring for their 'far out' clientele!"

Beverley Ann Beevers agreed:

> "The town was split into different groups at this time – the trendies, for want of a better word, and my group: the hippies – and rarely the two would sup in the same pub!

"One of our main pubs in the late '70s was the King George, run by Albion Turner and his wife Lolly. The King George was divided into four rooms, and different crowds kept to their own section. Ours was the jukebox room, and Albion was quick to scoot us out of the TV lounge room when the older end showed up to watch their horse racing. The divide always stayed firmly in place.

"'The George' was our base, and from here we ventured to Chennels, and the dark downstairs cellar bar in Old No 7, with its loud jukebox playing rock and folk music. We never went upstairs. We were packed in like sardines, but health and safety wasn't even a thing back then!

"The Temple bar up Graham's Orchard was a handy thoroughfare to Old No 7's back door, and from there it was on to The Travellers on Shambles Street. There was a saying in Barnsley, that if you had a beer in every pub along Shambles Street, you wouldn't reach the end.

"We also frequented The Wheatsheaf at townend on folk night, and The Vine up Pitt Street, with its welcoming coal fire in winter and a back room darker than the No 7's cellar bar. Wherever else we got to, last orders were always back in the George. Albion never served after time, so the bar was always six feet deep at ten to eleven, and if you didn't sup up by ten past, dear old Albi would escort you to the door – and through it!

"Then while the trendies went to Changes, and the older crowd to Ba-Ba, it was across the road to Stables for us, where we drank pints of Snakebite and Black Velvet and found ourselves truckin' – not dancing – into the early hours, barefoot on the dance floor, before picking the slivers of broken glass from our feet the next morning. Ayyy happy days..."

Enjoying drinks with friends was what the weekends were for

Every music-loving kid with money to spare, would at some point find themselves at Casa Disco, on Peel Square.

"It was a proper record store, the greatest record shop in Barnsley by far," said Ian McMillan

"That's where I bought my Captain Beefheart records. They had listening booths, and I remember once spending a full half hour in one of those booths listening to Colloseum's Valentyne Suite and then leaving without buying it. The guy who owned it wagged his finger at me as I walked out," he laughed.

"It was also one of those places that would have 'bass player wanted' signs up – a proper record shop. Neal's Music Store on the Arcade was another great one.

"It was also during the '70s when the BBC1 Radio roadshow came to town, I remember kids wagging off school to go. The Who were on amazingly, and then there were all these school kids who had shown up for the roadshow, so the audience was a sea of school uniforms!"

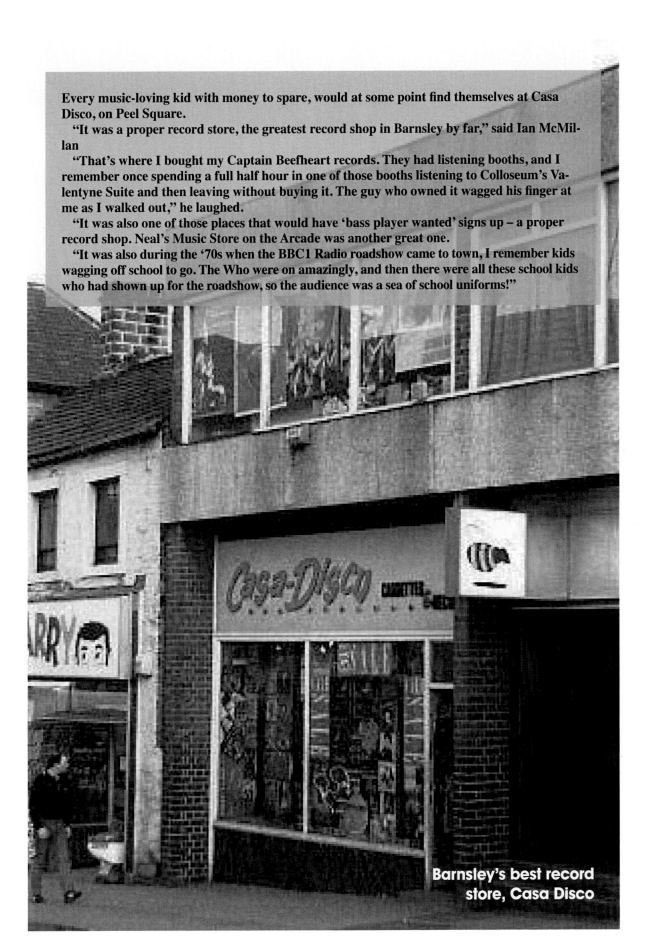

Barnsley's best record store, Casa Disco

Jim Sheridan, Sue Turfrey
and Trev Sutcliffe, in
The Fitz

Kick off
with a visit to

# CASA DISCO

CASA DISCO
PEEL SQUARE
BARNSLEY
TEL: BARNSLEY 87981

**The largest selection of
Records and Tapes
in the Area**

**Casa Disco opening,
Barnsley Chronicle
advert (inset)**

**Hanging out
in The Fitz, The
King George,
and Old No 7**

Pat Glover poses at the bar

"For many of us, those years were some of the best of our lives."

## The Record Bar
### 44, CHEAPSIDE, BARNSLEY.
(BETWEEN BOOTS & BIRDS)

## L.P'S FROM 49p EACH
### OR 5 FOR £2
100's OF OTHER BARGAINS

**RECORD BAR COUPON**

## 5p in £ OFF
ALL NORMAL PRICE
L.P's AND SINGLES
BY BRINGING IN THIS COUPON

BARNSLEY-BORN disc jockey Steve Hamon, who now works for Radio Leeds took time off on Saturday to open Casa Disco, a new record shop on Peel Street. Here Steve makes a sale to Shirley Johnson (17), and Wendy Richards (17) watched by Mr. Terry Wood, shop manager.

## THE RECORD BAR
### 44A CHEAPSIDE, BARNSLEY
(Between Boots and Birds)

**COMPETITION** Find a New name for our shop and win 3 L.P's of your choice

ALSO 2nd and 3rd PRIZES of SINGLES AND POSTERS

ALL ENTRIES TO BE SENT TO ABOVE ADDRESS

ALSO:—

BRING THIS COUPON IN AND SAVE 2½p ON SINGLES AND 10p ON ALL NORMAL PRICE L.P.'s

### Kick off with a visit to
# CASA DISCO

CASA DISCO
PEEL SQUARE
BARNSLEY
TEL: BARNSLEY 87981

**The largest selection of Records and Tapes in the Area**

**The Iron Mad Wilkinson Band play at The Globe in the early seventies**

**In the 70s, many women were turning to their sewing machines and copying dress patterns to create their own (cut-price) look!**

# Chapter 4
# Pollyanna, hot pants and poker straight hair

For Rita Britton, one aspect of the '70s still stands out clearly – the fashion.

"It was a whole new generation of fashion, quite revolutionary," she recalled with a smile.

"We were a lot more courageous in the way we dressed then than young people are today.

 Some of the outfits I wore – miniskirts and thigh boots – would literally stop the traffic. It was like a tsunami, all the young people were doing it and the young people of Barnsley were no exception.

The people of this small town embraced the glam decade in every way."

And, when it comes to fashion, Rita would know. She is the owner of clothing store Pollyanna which launched in Barnsley in 1967 and is the town's longest running independent store.

"I think 90 per cent of young people at that time shopped at my store, nobody travelled much then," said Rita.

"Pollyanna had five locations over the years, but the original shop, which opened in 1969, was in Shambles Street. I remember it had red flock wallpaper and gold paint, and windows that were virtually blacked out, so it was really dark inside, but that's

"Ashley Jackson did the sign writing for me on the first store, as that was his day job back then, and if you look closely at pictures of the shop then, you'll see that there's an L missing from the name. I didn't notice it until later, or I'd have asked him to re-do it, so it stayed like that for a long time.

what all the shops did at that time.

"I had wall lights up, but you really couldn't see at all. And there was no telephone then, so people just showed up.

"Inside the store, I only had two rails of clothing, stocking names like Mary Quant and Ozzy Clarke. It was a different time then, there wasn't the competition there is now; no internet, no Selfridges, no Harrods.

"I remember doing fashion shows at Club Ba-Ba, and thinking it was like something out of a James Bond movie, with the casino, and all the big names and acts of the time appearing.

"One evening, after one of our fashion shows, the owner Peter Casson invited us to go and have a meal in the restaurant upstairs when we were finished and we were all completely in awe, on our best behaviour and trying our best to act like we belonged in somewhere so fine. It was fantastic.

"I was 26 when I launched Pollyanna. I think young people were altogether more aspirational then than they are now. There was definitely this feeling amongst the young people that we could do or be anything we wanted to be.

"It was a wealthy town back then too, because the miners were earning really good wages, and so their families had money to spend.

"Ours was the first generation to be earning and spending our own money. Before that, girls would dress as their mother did; they'd buy a suit from the Coop and wear it with three-quarter length gloves that matched their shoes and the cover on their umbrella.

"It was only when we got the northern bands coming along that the cultural revolution began. I don't think you can separate fashion and music; each one influences the other. The independents, like mine, started this new wave, stocking the new designers first, and it took the bigger department stores longer to take the risk and get on board.

"It was a rebellion! Suddenly everywhere you looked, there were hot pants, patent leather boots, miniskirts and flared jeans."

Jan Hollingsworth said: "I loved the hot pants, the knee length platform boots, the brogues, the Levi's and the edge-stitched shirts with rounded collars.

"I bought a lot of my clothes at Chelsea Girl, on the high street."

Sandra Price said:

"The '70s was all about baggy trousers, high waistbands and denim waistcoats."

Joyce Beevers said: "Women really loved wearing their finery on a night out in the '70s; it was more about really just loving doing it back then, of enjoying dressing up."

Linda Hammond said: "We all used to shop at Pollyanna in the '70s, my sister Margaret more than anyone, she'd spend all her money there!

"I once bought a suede two-piece from Rita that my daughter Amy still has to this day. It was a pencil skirt, black suede with a grey suede slit up the side, and a black waistcoat with grey trim.

"I still also have a pair of patterned knickerbocker trousers from Pollyanna in my wardrobe that are nearly 50 years old. I saved them because they were what I was wearing on my first date with my now-husband John, in 1971. I remember wearing them with a black polo neck shirt, pink suede waistcoat, and pink suede boots, and thinking I was the bee's knees!

"It was a fantastic place to shop, Rita was always

**Rita Britton, pictured in the early days of Pollyanna**

right on top of the fashions."

Rita continued: "I once travelled down from Barnsley to watch an Ozzy Clarke show in London and bought a sample pair of patent leather boots that I thought were just the best things since sliced bread. The problem was I couldn't get them off when I got back to the hotel, so I had to get in the bath in them, with my legs dangling over the side!

"'70s fashion started out quite exciting, but towards the end I think it all became a bit ugly, and all the men started looking like Jason King, with their droopy moustaches, fat ties, and flared jeans – horrible!"

Barnsley bard, Ian Macmillan, said: "I remember I had long hair by 1970, and was wearing flared trousers. We weren't allowed beards at school, but we were allowed sideburns, so my friends and I were walking around school looking like Noddy Holder. We really thought being hairy was the thing!"

Chris Evans said: "I remember feeling very smart in my dark brown mohair suit, complete with curly braid, dress shirt and brown velvet dicky bowtie."

Rita added: "We also saw hemlines go from one extreme to the other, starting with tiny miniskirts, and seeing them drop all the way down with the maxi dresses.

"I also remember I had long hair that I ironed dry on the ironing board, placing brown paper over it, and then ironing it poker straight. It's crazy when you think about it now.

"I bought some Levi's in the '70s, and the big thing to do at that time was get in the bath with them on so that they'd shrink right down to a skintight fit. That was fine as long as you kept your jeans on, because your legs would be stained blue underneath them! When it came time to put them back on, you had to lie on the floor and concave your stomach so that you could zip them up. Crazy times."

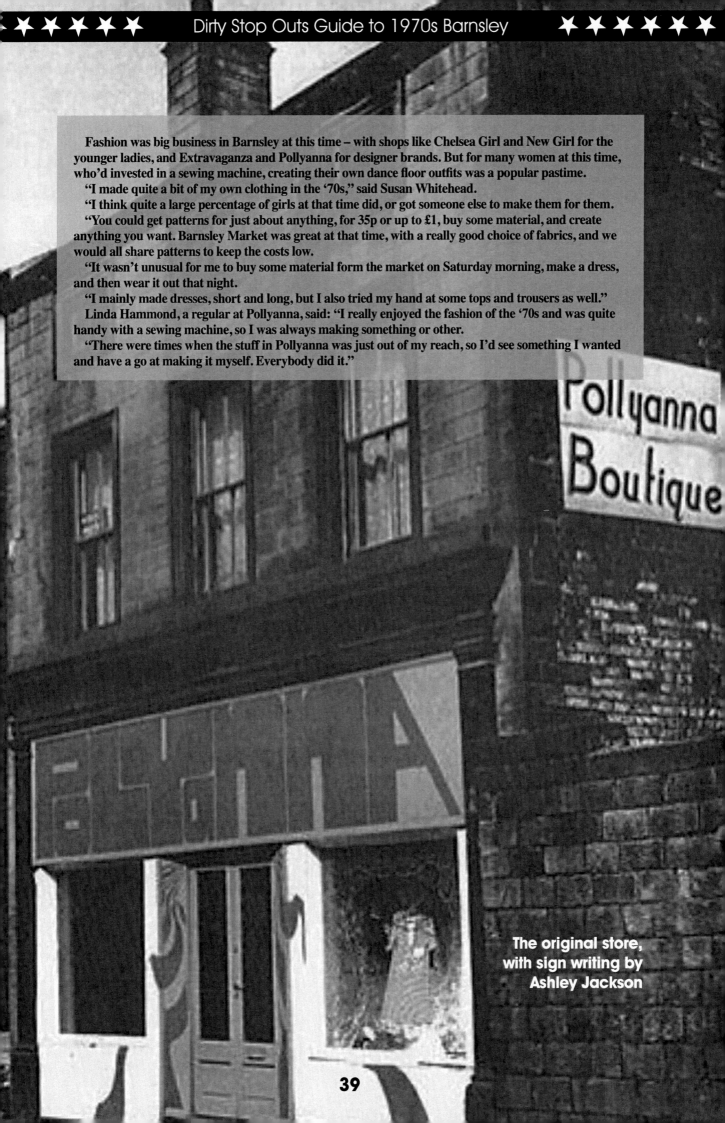

Fashion was big business in Barnsley at this time – with shops like Chelsea Girl and New Girl for the younger ladies, and Extravaganza and Pollyanna for designer brands. But for many women at this time, who'd invested in a sewing machine, creating their own dance floor outfits was a popular pastime.

"I made quite a bit of my own clothing in the '70s," said Susan Whitehead.

"I think quite a large percentage of girls at that time did, or got someone else to make them for them.

"You could get patterns for just about anything, for 35p or up to £1, buy some material, and create anything you want. Barnsley Market was great at that time, with a really good choice of fabrics, and we would all share patterns to keep the costs low.

"It wasn't unusual for me to buy some material form the market on Saturday morning, make a dress, and then wear it out that night.

"I mainly made dresses, short and long, but I also tried my hand at some tops and trousers as well."

Linda Hammond, a regular at Pollyanna, said: "I really enjoyed the fashion of the '70s and was quite handy with a sewing machine, so I was always making something or other.

"There were times when the stuff in Pollyanna was just out of my reach, so I'd see something I wanted and have a go at making it myself. Everybody did it."

**The original store, with sign writing by Ashley Jackson**

Maggie Hammond
and friend in dresses
from Pollyanna

Pat Glover recalls putting things on layaway in Chelsea Girl, and then paying them off over the course of a few weeks.

"That was something else we all did," she laughed.

"Shops like Chelsea Girl understood that girls like me, students with Saturday jobs, didn't have a lot of money, so they would allow girls to put a deposit of a few pounds on something and then pay it off over a month or so.

"It wasn't like today, when people can afford to buy so many things they don't even get around to wearing half of it. We'd covet something, put a deposit on it, pay it off over a few weeks and it was so exciting the day we were finally able to pick it up and wear it out. Then proceeded to wear it to death! The great thing was that then, it was yours, you'd earned it, you'd worked for it. We took a lot of pride in and care of things.

"It was such an exciting time for fashion, and long before the days of the internet, girls like me would see a photograph in a magazine, and see a hairstyle or someone's makeup that we liked, and we'd save the page, stick it up on our mirror and do our best to replicate it on our next night out.

"Trends spread because everyone saw things they liked on other people and copied. It was brilliant fun."

Ladies dolled up and having fun at Rebeccas nightclub

For men too, hair in the '70s got bigger

'70s fashion was bold and brave

41

LAST £.s.d. SALE
CONTINUES AT
EXTRAVAGANZA
BOUTIQUE
PEEL STREET ARCADE, BARNSLEY
Dresses, Coats, Trouser Suits,
Children's Wear, Blouses, Tunics
ALL GARMENTS REDUCED TO
UNBELIEVABLE PRICES—
MANY AT COST
SPECIAL OFFER THIS SAT. ONLY—
FREE PAIR TOP QUALITY TIGHTS
with every garment purchased

GENTLEMEN, just what you have been waiting for . . . Linda and Chris are waiting to measure and fit you with all the latest men's wear, shirts, jackets and suits which they have in stock at the new Claptrap boutique in Sheffield Road.

HURRY!
BUTTERFIELDS
WINTER SALE
NOW IN FULL SWING

"DIMENSIONS" clients Stuart Jagger (14) and Pamela Dewhirst show off their hairstyles while John Major (right) and Bill Shaw (left) admire their own handiwork.

**Josephine Turner reviewing
tights, with tights survey
man, Chris Davidson**

**Rocking short skirts and short hair, early in the 70s**

**Big hair was the thing in the 70s – whatever your gender!**

Stan Jnr poses with comedian Colin Crompton

# Chapter 5
## A town in pictures...

**S**tan Bulmer – it's a name most Barnsley people know well.

For 40 years Stan was the town's unofficial resident photographer, spending 25 years at The Barnsley Chronicle as its chief photographer and, later, joining his son, Stan Jnr, at their photographic studio, Stan Plus Stan Two.

Between them, the two Stans documented decades of town life, and their private archive is a veritable treasure trove of images from the decade of glam.

> "My dad never went anywhere without his camera around his neck,"

confirmed Stan, who officially launched the studio with his dad in 1978, when he was aged just 22, though the pair had been taking photographs together for years before that.

"He was much-loved in this town - everybody called his name when he was out and about, there wasn't a pub in the town he couldn't get an af-ter-hours drink in, and they even sang his name at Barnsley FC matches – 'Stan, Stan, give us a wave!'"

"We have thousands of negatives with all kinds of treasures on them from the 1970s, boxes and boxes full. When I looked back through them recently, it was incredible to recall some of the events we attended and the people we photographed. It was a brilliant time for us.

"My mum, Ada, worked at the Odeon cinema in town during the '70s. My dad would often be out working until 10pm, when my mum's shift finished, then go pick her up and the two of them would go out gallivanting for the night, to Ba-Ba, or later, after Ba-Ba's closed, to Rebeccas.

"Everybody loved my mum and had such a soft spot for my dad. Once I was old enough, I'd join them and was soon drawn into that clique; It was quite normal for me, socialising with my parents, it's just what I'd always done and we had a really good relationship.

"My dad knew every landlord that did 'after-time,'

**45**

**Emmerdale favourite, and Barnsley resident, Stan Richards tickling the ivories in a local pub – a favourite pastime of his**

he took his camera everywhere because he didn't want to miss anything; he never stopped.

"People were forever shouting him when he passed them on the street - as I said, everyone knew him - and the most popular cry was 'Stan, where are my bloody pictures?'" Stan laughed.

"He'd take photos of everything, but people rarely got the pictures he'd promised them, I suppose it was hard to keep track with all those negatives, it wasn't as simple then as it is now.

"My mum loved to go through old photos, especially after my dad was gone. She'd pull them all out and show me the different things they'd done and places they'd been."

and he loved a drink, so if it was Sunday, he'd say 'let's go see Mel at Horse and Jockey…' etc.

"We used to see Stan Richards out quite a lot too, from Emmerdale, as he was local. He was a pianist and comedian as well as an actor and could often be found playing the piano in some bar or other."

Pat Dowle, who was a regular on the Barnsley club scene in the '70s, said:

"I remember Stan and his wife out in Ba-Ba most weekends, and his camera was always slung around his neck, he was never without it."

Joyce Beever said: "Stan Bulmer took all of my photos in the '70s, he and his wife were terrific. Ada and Stan came as a couple, always, and they loved to socialise – but Stan was never without his camera! Ada was lovely, she'd always let us slip into the Odeon for free."

Though Stan and his wife have since passed away, Stan Jnr says their spirit lives on in the disorganized bundle of thousands of negatives and prints that capture some of their happiest years and memories, living and working as a young couple in the town they loved.

"My dad loved having his photograph taken," said Stan, who says he grew up surrounded by pictures and cameras, and bought his first camera for £25 in the '70s, to start working with his dad.

"And he absolutely loved taking pictures; it was never just a job to him, it was who he was. I believe

And Stan says the '70s was a great time in Barnsley, with key events that still stand out to this day.

"The big thing about Barnsley in the '70s was obviously the pits, and the fact that everybody who wanted a job, had a job, everyone who wanted an apprenticeship, had an apprenticeship," said Stan.

"I remember Alan Clarke coming to Barnsley FC, that was quite significant at the time. There were the street parties for the Silver Jubilee, and I remember my dad photographing the annual LVA presentations, that really were the social event of the year. He and I both photographed Shaun Doyle's boxing nights, which were just incredible, as there was nothing else like them being done in South Yorkshire at that time and everybody who was anybody turned out for them. I remember photographing The Birdcage in Hoyland, parties at Keresforth Hall and Ardsley House, and the Mayor's Parades.

"I met a lot of the big names of the time too – Charlie Williams, Dickie Bird, Tony Christie, Ronnie Dukes and Ricki Lee, plus a lot of the footballers.

"There were so many pubs in those days, and I drank in town back then, so the White Hart and Old No 7 were regular haunts for me. Towards the end of the '70s, I worked as a photographer at Rebeccas, and would often jump behind the bar to help out when it got busy. They were great times.

"Building wise the town has changed immensely in the past 40 years, but the people of Barnsley are just the same as they always have been, warm and friendly. I'm proud to be a part of such a great town."

Les Dawson cosies up to Stan's wife, Ada Bulmer, in the changing rooms at Keresforth Hall

Stan with comedian Paul Shane

"Who doesn't remember the Barnsley Chronicle's Girl Fridays?" smiled Stan.

"Each week the Chronicle would feature a different local girl – from beauty queens to office workers – and I recall that some of them were pretty racy, to say it's a family newspaper. I can still see some of the pictures now!

"My dad, as the Chronicle's official photographer, photographed many of the girls, in their hot pants, and their bikinis, all over the town. I seem to remember it caused the odd argument with my mum!"

**Stan Snr attended many of the LVA trips as part of his photographic duties, at which the alcohol flowed freely!**

**Shaun Doyle and Dickie Bird with pals'**

**A group enjoy the festivities at the regular boxing night**

**Shaun Doyle's legendary boxing nights**

There were celebrations held all across the town, to mark the Queen's Silver Jubilee. Stan Snr is pictured in the middle of the festivities

Ada Bulmer (centre) poses backstage with a young Tony Christie

Michael Parkinson pops by to visit Club Ba-Ba on a visit to the town, along with Stan Snr

Amongst the familiar faces are Colin Crompton, Ronnie Dukes, Stan Richards and Charlie Williams

Stan Jnr (centre), camera in hand, enjoying a night with pals at Rebecca's nightclub in the late 70s'

Ada on duty at The Barnsley Odeon, where she worked before moving on to The Ritz

**The Barnsley Bitter
Protest of '74**

# Chapter 6

## It's a case of 'beer in, brains out' with legendary Barnsley Bitter!

**W**hether it's the seductive Barnsley Bitter, the hearty Barnsley Chop, or the infamous Barnsley Marathon, this proud mining town has never been afraid to stamp its ownership on a quality product, event or - in the case of Barnsley Bard, Ian McMillan – person.

Which is why 1976 marked the very sad end of an era, as the last barrels of Barnsley Bitter were loaded and shipped out of the town's Oakwell-based brewery.

The town had fought tooth and nail to keep production of the legendary brew going, ever since the brewery's closure was first proposed in 1970.

> 'Barnsley drinkers developed a bitter taste in their mouths this week with the news that the production of Barnsley Bitter is to be phased out in the next three years,'
> The Barnsley Chronicle confirmed on February 23, 1973.

'Barnsley Bitter has always been known as a Northerner's drink. People used to say that once you had tasted Oakwell Ales you couldn't stand to drink anything else.'

The folk of Barnsley fought back against the announcement. When petitions alone failed to make an impact, the Barnsley Bitter Protest March of '74 was arranged, which saw hundreds of locals, as well as Campaign for Real Ale drinkers from all across the country, take to the town's streets that September, visiting and drinking at each of the Barnsley pubs that still sold Barnsley Bitter.

"I remember that march well," said Beverley Ann Beevers.

"I was bringing up the rear with my best buddy Mag Jones, and the march was on the *News at ten* that night.

"A couple of things though - I was only 17 when I went on the march, and Mags and I were both carrying bottles of cider. Oops!"

But despite a long battle, that even saw the 'save Barnsley Brewery' cause make its way to the House of Commons, thanks to local MP, and Defence Secretary, Roy Mason, who considered Barnsley Bitter 'the best brew in England,' the fight was eventually lost.

UNDER A.A.A. & W.C.C.R.W.A. LAWS

# Barnsley & South Yorkshire Championship

# MARATHON

## 26 miles
### 385 yards

| START AND FINISH | BARNSLEY TOWN HALL |
|---|---|

# Sunday 2nd December 1979

### Start 12 noon / Finish 2·15 onwards

ROUTE: Church St, Gawber Rd, Pogmoor Rd, Broadway, Ward Green, Worsbrough Dale, Stairfoot, Wombwell, Brampton, Wath & Bolton upon Dearne. Return same route.

## Organised by Barnsley Road Runners Club

### Sponsored by Barnsley Chronicle and South Yorkshire ⬡ County Council

**Celebrating with a well-earned drink after finishing the Barnsley Six marathon**

Roy Mason was quoted at the time as saying: "I hope that the unions, Barnsley Bitter drinkers and publicans will fight to save Barnsley's best beer and, in the end, if Barnsley Bitter goes, then the message is don't drink John Smith's."

Dave Cherry said: "Barnsley Bitter, what a drink. You could smell the hops in it, very strong smell, and it always had a frothy top. The saying was 'it's like brandy.'

"We'd go out 'rarnd tarn' drinking, then five o'clock the next day we were up for the pit – it was a bad mix. It was around then I first heard the saying 'beer in, brains out'."

Steve Crossland said: "I enjoyed Barnsley Bitter back in the day, a very bitter drink indeed."

Keith Parr recalled: "If memory serves, The Trades Club on Racecommon Road was one of the last places to sell Barnsley Bitter. I was a member there from the age of 16."

Melv Kirkham said: "Barnsley Bitter was like Sam Smiths, either you liked it or you didn't. I definitely had a few of them…"

Margaret Smith, who ran The Cross Keys pub in the town centre, agreed: "It was a medium beer that clung to the glass all the way down. We sold gallons of the stuff."

Barbara Lloyd said: "Brilliant beer, but then again, they knew how to keep beer right in those days, proper pub landlords."

Heather Gambler said: "We had a northern lad in the pro band I was in, in 1973/74. We worked on a cruise ship and, on one of the Canary Islands, he was shouting 'Barnsley Bitter!' to passers-by from the taxi window. He also included it in an entertainment crew rendition of 'If I were not upon the stage… a barman I would be, you'd hear me all day long singing out this song, Barnsley Bitter, Barnsley Bitter, I'd be drunk all day…' etc."

1973 also signalled the first ever Barnsley Mayor's Parade, with thousands of people packing into the town centre on a cloudy Saturday July 14, to celebrate the debut event, organised by the Junior Chamber of Commerce.

A report in The Barnsley Chronicle the following Friday July 20 read: 'Crowds of flag-waving children lined the streets, while workers hung from office windows and jammed shop doorways in an effort not to miss any of the show.

'The theme of the parade was 'Barnsley 73,' but floats varied from an Indian camp, complete with totem pole, to a moon rocket.

'Highlight of the afternoon was a fly-past by four Jet Provosts from RAF Leeming, which swooped low and flew in formation over the town several times.

'For two hours, police kept traffic at bay while the parade, comprising nearly 70 floats and bands, wound its way through the town centre, living up to its promise of being a sparkling affair.'

Another prominent event in the town's history was the launch of the now legendary Barnsley Six Marathon in 1974, organised by Barnsley Road Runners Club. It attracted hundreds of athletes from all over Britain, and saw thousands more local people take up running in a bid to compete for the top prize.

Frank Higham and his pal, Martin Storr, decided to enter the race for a bet after a few beers one night in the Wilthorpe Hotel.

 "We were bet eight pints each by our mates that we would not finish the race," said Frank.

"I was officially placed last and was presented with a tie by the Mayor on the Barnsley Town Hall steps. I still have the tie."

The pair quickly fell to the back, with eventually only a police motorcyclist to accompany them around the course. As the boys headed to the finish line, the spectators parted to let them through, rallying around to cheer them on and across the line.

The following year, the race went down in the British Athletics history books for being the first marathon in the country in which women were allowed to take part.

The women's crown on the day went to 22-year-old Hilary Matthews, who crossed the finish line in three hours, 13 minutes and 27 seconds, beating 36 of the male contestants

Amanda West said: "I remember sitting on the wall outside the miners' offices, on the corner of Huddersfield Road, to watch the Barnsley marathon."

Dave Allemby said: "Sadly it would be impossible to do this same course nowadays. It used to be the biggest marathon in the country before the London Marathon started in 1981. Happy days."

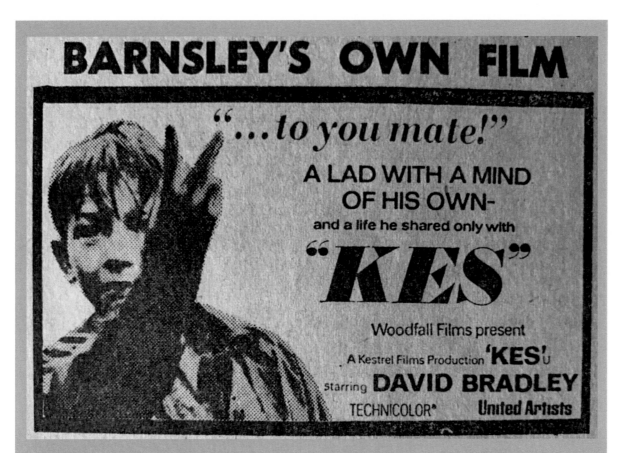

Kes was released in Barnsley in March 1970, and thrust the town into the spotlight.

"It was, of course, all filmed locally, with genuine Barnsley people, and there was a lot of controversy at the time about the use of the working class dialect," said Dave Cherry.

"There was some conjecture that it should be dubbed, but they ended up keeping it as it is. And thank goodness they did, Kes was a phenomenal success when it was released, putting the town firmly on the map."

Linda Hammond, a go-go dancer at Club Ba-Ba in the early '70s, said: "My brother and sister and I all attended auditions for the film at The Queen's Hotel, at the bottom of Eldon Street North.

"My brother Bob, who worked on the club circuit for years as a ventriloquist, under the name 'Tony and Grandad,' auditioned for Judd, but apparently he didn't come across as aggressive enough for the part.

"My sister Maggie and I were both up for the part of 'the legs in the library.' They were looking for a studious librarian type, and I'd just come back from working in the Channel Islands, all super-tanned, with freckles and this wild red hair," she laughed.

"Maggie was far more pasty and studious-looking, the total opposite to me. She wound up getting the part.

"I remember when the film was released and we all went along to watch it, it was so exciting, just waiting to spy Maggie's legs! So many people we knew went along to watch the film just to spy a glimpse of my sister's legs – 'there they are, look!' we'd all shout, when they came on the screen. It was brilliant."

**The famous Barnsley Six Marathon, which launched in 1974**

**The popular Barnsley cycle race**

**A copy of Athletics Weekly, crowning Hilary Matthews the winner of the female runners: a historic moment for British Athletics**

An early Barnsley Mayor's Parade in full swing!

53

SUFFER
THE LITTLE
CHILDREN

53

**Barnsley's annual Mayor's Parades launched in the town in 1973**

# Chapter 7

## Taking a 'turn' around the town's clubs

❝The working mens' club scene is a pale shadow now of what it used to be," says Dave Cherry, who played with a number of bands throughout the '60s and '70s, including the Levvy Taggers and The Dolphins.**

"It was absolutely on fire in the '70s. There were some really big clubs at that time. I played at Barnsley Radical and Liberal Club, a big town centre venue that had acts on five nights a week, and dancing on a Monday.

❝ If you weren't in the Liberal by half past seven, you didn't get a seat. The atmosphere in there was electric!

"There was The Trades of course too, at town end, which always had live music.

"The Corner Pin was another one, and it would be absolutely heaving on a Saturday afternoon. It was only a small place, but vibrant.

❝ "Barnsley audiences were notoriously hard to please. They'd sit there with their arms folded: 'entertain me,' that wa' rubbish,' 'turn it down a bit,' 'we want thee off before t'bingo starts!'"

"The Ba-Ba Club was a real high-class place to play, Friday night was always heaving. We were always the second act and we got to play on the same bill as some big names.

"The Civic Hall was another great one; Monday night was the teen-and-twenty club and that was always a lot of fun. I'll never forget one night I was singing Chuck Berry's *Too Much Monkey Business* and, halfway through verse four, the words went completely out of my head; I could have crawled

**Enjoying a spot of Bells!**

into a hole, it was horrible!

"The Wine Shades was great on a Saturday and Sunday night, jam-packed and with a great atmosphere. I remember we got about £8 for the group.

"The Georges was another good one we did regular. There was also an early afternoon club, called KJH, down a little ginnel in Peel Square, and it was the only place you could get an afternoon drink in those days.

"Later in the '70s I started going out singing on my own, doing some Barry Manilow, Beatles, Hollies, and Shadows stuff. I could easily get four or five bookings a week, just working my way around the pubs and clubs in the local area. I'd get home from a gig at 2am, then be up for my job, as an electrician in the pits, at 5am. It was hard graft, living two lives in parallel, but a lot of fun.

"One place I did a few times was the Yorkshire Traction 'Tracky' club, on Harborough Hills, and they had Sunday afternoon strippers on, which was always chockablock. I've always been a happily married man, so it was never my cup of tea, but when you were playing there, they'd ask you to playing background music, to back the strippers while they did their thing. You didn't know where to put your eyes!"

Terry Herrington worked as musician throughout the '70s, with a brief stint at Club Ba-Ba in the early

seventies, before joining Ronnie Dukes and Ricki Lee's act later in the decade.

> Clubs like that just don't exist anymore. Kids today don't know what a real nightclub is.

"Club Ba-Ba was great," he recalled.

"A really nice nightclub, with fantastic silver service restaurant and great cabaret. I worked there as musical director for a couple of years, so I'd start the night playing piano near the stage, while people were arriving and getting their tables. Then I'd move on to the organ, to play for the show and the cabaret, until about quarter to twelve. At that point I'd be joined by another five or six musicians, and we'd play music for everyone to dance to until about 2am. And this was seven nights a week! It was a great privilege to work with so many fantastic acts.

"The clubs were people's social time, they were the weekends for them, so they were vibrant and bustling. An act in the working mens' clubs at this time could work every night of the week, the whole year round, and not repeat the same club twice in the year."

Shirley Musgrave said: "The main crime, when we travelled the clubs with my late husband and Pagan Chorus, was your choice of seats, e.g. 'don't sit there, Mrs-so-and-so likes to be near the bingo caller, or the toilets, or the bar, and that's their regular seat!' We daren't sit down anywhere until we'd checked. And if you dared to win the bingo or raffles - escape quickly!

**Husband and wife variety act, Ronnie Dukes and Ricki Lee, enjoying themselves in the clubs during a Skol promotion**

**The Barnsley entertainment pair cosy up to bar staff during a local gig**

**1970 production of Little Red Riding Hood at Barnsley Civic Theatre**